Victorian and Edwardian
NORFOLK

from old photographs

1   The Great Yarmouth Fishermen's Hospital was built in the Market Place in 1702. 'This picturesque court, with its Dutch gables and pantile roofs, old thin bricks and dormer windows, with mullioned windows on the ground floor and classical pediment to the inner gateway, marks the transitional period between Jacobean and Georgian at the beginning of the eighteenth century'. (Ecclestone, A. W., and J. L., *The rise of Great Yarmouth*, p. 172.) Photo: P. H. Emerson (1887)

2   (*overleaf*) Norwich City macebearers at the end of the nineteenth century. The mace on the left was presented to the City by Sir Robert Walpole in 1733, and the Sword of State and all the badges by the St. George's Company in 1705. The two chains formerly belonged to the City waits or minstrels

Victorian and Edwardian

NORFOLK

from old photographs

Introduction and commentaries by

PHILIP HEPWORTH

B. T. BATSFORD LTD

LONDON

Printed in Great Britain by
William Clowes & Sons, Limited
London, Beccles and Colchester
for the Publishers B. T. Batsford Ltd
4 Fitzhardinge Street, London W1H 0AH

First published in 1972
ISBN 0 7134 0124 9
Text copyright © Philip Hepworth 1972

Though Norffolk thus all other shires excell
In all that serve for belly, back, or health
Or pleasure, ease, or strength foe to repell
Yet other shires som compt of greater welth
For that theire lande Revenue yieldeth moare
& do not breed so great excess of poore

Henry Gurney (1548–1615)

By the same author

Archives and Manuscripts in Libraries
How to Find Out in History
Select Biographical Sources

3 On the beach, 1894

CONTENTS

ACKNOWLEDGMENTS

The Author and Publishers would like to thank the following for permission to reproduce photographs: The Earl of Albemarle (93); David E. Bowskill (54, 73–75, 80, 103, 143, 145, 154); Mr R. Spayne of Bowyer & Spayne Ltd. (149); Mr L. G. Butcher of J. J. Colman (92); Colman Library (19, 113, 119, 129, 139, 151); Mrs Elizabeth Dutton (110); Sir Bartle Edwards (93, 94); Eastern Counties Newspapers, the Norwich Collection of G. E. Swain (59, 152, 153, 160); Mr J. Easton (112); Alderman T. C. Eaton (5, 6, 11); Mr Leslie Fenn (146); Miss K. Hall (78); Mr Bryan Hall (8, 60, 67, 86, 91, 121, 132, 157); Lady Harrod (57, 87–89, 118, 131, 141, 162); Mr D. H. Heath (90); Mr C. Crawford Holden (62, 63, 65, 79, 104); Mr Raymond Wilson of King's Lynn Public Library (36, 81, 142, 144, 148); Miss J. M. Kennedy of the Norfolk & Norwich Record Office (28, 32, 39, 40, 53, 93, 136, 150); Mr Francis Cheetham of the Norwich Museums (15, 44, 55, 98, 100, 116, 120, 127, 130); Radio Times Hulton Picture Library (84, 96); Rye Library (1, 2, 7, 9, 10, 13, 14, 16–18, 20–27, 30, 33, 38, 45–50, 52, 56, 58, 68, 70–72, 76, 85, 97, 99, 101, 102, 105, 107, 108, 111, 114, 115, 117, 122, 126, 128, 133–135, 137, 138, 140, 147, 158, 159, 161); Smith Collection (12, 29, 37, 51, 64, 77, 82, 83, 123, 124); Mr H. T. G. Tinkler (34, 43); Victoria & Albert Museum (106, 155). The Colman Library, Rye Library and Smith collections are part of the Norwich Public Libraries collection. The remaining photographs are from the Publisher's collection.

INTRODUCTION

4 Home from school, 1894

PHOTOGRAPHIC SURVEYS

Librarians were in the field with photographic surveys long before the planners and the dons. The earliest local photographic survey, of Warwickshire, was founded by W. Jerome Harrison and Sir Benjamin Stone following a paper read by the former to the Birmingham Photographic Society in 1889. In 1958 ten municipal libraries (Croydon, Leyton, Norwich, Nottingham, Birmingham, Cardiff, Hereford, Manchester, Leeds and Warrington) housed more than 10,000 photographic prints, and by 1970 this figure had grown to 52 libraries. Not all these acquired their photographs through a formal survey, and perhaps the most systematic work done locally today is in Worcestershire, where the County Archivist commissions amateurs to photograph named localities.

There are in addition to these local topographical surveys national subject collections such as that of the British Transport Commission, London; the Museum of Rural Life, Reading University (agriculture), and the National Monuments Record. The Victoria and Albert and Science Museums hold large photographic collections and the commercial productions of Aerofilms Ltd., and the Radio Times Hulton Picture Library are of great importance.

In 1897 the National Photographic Record Association was founded on the initiative of Sir Benjamin Stone (1838–1914), and prints from the resulting survey were stored in the Department of Prints and Drawings in the British Museum after the dissolution of the Association in 1910. Stone's own collections were deposited in the Birmingham Reference Library, where I used to browse among them while waiting for a train after a weekly lecturing appointment I held there immediately after the Second World War. It was these prints and Stone's two-volume work published in 1906, with its scenes of English customs, ranging from Abbots Bromley's Horn Dance to the Pancake tossing at Westminster School, that first impressed me with the value of recording the wealth of English customs and ceremonies.

Less than 40% of the local British library photographic collections are based on an organised survey, many including the type of photograph amusingly described by Roger Ellis as those collected by a typical old-style librarian: 'a collection of photographs, of local worthies, local occasions (such as the visits of Garibaldi and the Shah of Persia) and . . . of buildings about to be demolished. It is true that [the librarian] did not intentionally photograph any buildings of later date than 1714, but the later ones generally got into the photographs by accident and are now the most interesting part.'

THE COLLECTIONS AT NORWICH

The Norwich collection was originally based on a survey, which now, apart from the current accessions of prints submitted to the Local Photographic Society's Record Class competition, depends on fortuitous donations, or special commissioning of records of buildings about to be demolished. The Survey was inaugurated in 1913 following what turned out to be a very successful attempt at a complete photographic record of the disastrous Norwich flood of August 1912. The report of the then City Librarian, G. A. Stephen, on the reasons for the Survey cannot be bettered: 'Few counties offer so rich a field for photographic survey work as that of Norfolk; its wealth of old domestic buildings and churches, and its castles, abbeys and priories, are interesting for their historical associations or their architectural beauties; its geological deposits and ancient earthworks attract the geologist and palaeontologist; its varied flora and fauna delight the naturalist; while the beauties of its pastoral scenery, Broadland, Poppyland, and its sea-coast resorts give pleasure to all persons who love picturesque scenery. All these subjects, as well as civic functions, important ceremonies, and passing events, provide material which is worthy of being photographed and permanently preserved for general use.'

L. Stanley Jast (1868–1949), who had inaugurated a Surrey Survey as Chief Librarian of Croydon, and was in 1916 the co-author of what is still the standard book on photographic surveys, came to Norwich to promote the Survey which staged its first public exhibition less than a year before the outbreak of World War 1. The 1500 prints of 1913, of which 200 were displayed at the exhibition had grown to over 20,000 by 1971, not including two further sources in the Norwich Public Libraries drawn upon for this book. A collection of 7,000 Norfolk prints acquired by Walter Rye (1834–1929), the Norfolk antiquary, from J. Smith of Regent Street, London, in 1896, and presented to the

Norwich Public Libraries in 1905–6, includes many hundreds of old photographs never separately recorded. 1200 Norfolk photographic prints from the firm F. Frith and Co., Reigate, were acquired in 1970 with the help of a grant from the Friends of the National Libraries; they are particularly strong on the coastal resorts and market towns not well covered elsewhere in the Libraries. The old-established Colman and Rye Libraries of Local History, Norwich, particularly the former, include numerous albums of photographs, *cartes-de-visite,* and a good number of printed volumes with pasted-in photographs, and Norfolk and its region has had more than its fair share of lavish photographically illustrated guide books of the type of the *Eastern Counties Pictorial Guide,* 'containing nearly 200 views of East Anglia, price 1/–', (Bright's, Bournemouth, 1899), or biographies such as *Men who have made Norwich* (Burgess, 1904), containing interior industrial scenes.

The Norfolk and Norwich Record Office (founded 1963) in the same building as the Central Library, has also accumulated, when included in other deposits, a few interesting collections of old photographs.

PHOTOGRAPHY IN NORFOLK

Norfolk was early on the photographic scene. Mrs Anne Rigby, wife of a well-known Norwich physician and mother-in-law of Sir Charles Eastlake, first President of the London (later Royal) Photographic Society from 1853, was photographed in 1845 by David Octavius Hill of Edinburgh (1802–70) whose work is mentioned in C. S. Minto's companion *Victorian and Edwardian Scotland from old photographs.* In Norwich Roger's 1859 directory lists ten 'photographic artists' including Sawyer and Co. of 42 London Street, whose cabinet-sized portraits proved very popular in succeeding decades. Years later J. R. Sawyer of this firm established at Ealing an autotype works, and in 1887 he described his process, which transposed tolerable reproductions of photographs directly on to pages; previously they had to be stuck individually into books. The advertisement of Rogers and Havers, 5 Davey Place in the 1859 directory promised stereoscopic views and the copying of faded daguerreotypes. Harrod's 1863 directory of Norfolk advertised Jeary's album portraits: 'R. J. fearlessly invites comparison with any in the world'. At the Corn Hall, Diss, on March 1st 1859, took place 'an evening in Palestine . . . by means of the Magic lantern; an exhibition of dissolving views from Frith's celebrated photographs of the Holy Land.' Some 60 views, 'each view will cover a disc of nearly 100 square feet', were shown and admission ranged from reserved seats at 1/6, 'family tickets to admit six, 7/6' to promenade 3d. By 1865 Kelly's directory of Norfolk records 18 Norwich photographers, five in Great Yarmouth, three in King's Lynn and one in London. In 1869 the Norwich firm of Burgess and Grimwood advertised the 'Eburneum process' of mounting photographs in an improved style. Long before this, Richard Beard, who had started the first professional studio for daguerreotypes in Europe in London in 1841, had opened up in Norwich in 1843, and amateurs were practising the calotype form of photography as early as 1845, notably Mr J. Blowers of Costessey, stated some ten years later to be 'the oldest of our local amateurs', when there was in being a Norwich Photographic Society, founded in 1854. This, the fourth oldest in the English provinces, was discontinued in 1861. Leading members were Dr James Howes, G. R. Fitt, J. R. Sawyer and the President, Thomas Damant Eaton (1800-71) (5), three of whose albums of calotypes have survived. He produced illustration 11. Many of his shots were taken in and around his garden in Chapel Field, Norwich. Frederic Scott Archer, inaugurator of the wet collodion process, soon to supersede the calotype (see below), and the daguerreotype which produced one positive only on metal, only to be duplicated by rephotography, exhibited some studies of clouds and landscape at the Society's first exhibition (November 1856–February 1857). G. R. Fitt (illus. 10, 17), 'to whose instruction and example the society was much indebted in its infancy', is also represented in the printed catalogue. The calotype process, invented by W. H. Fox Talbot in 1834 and used for a minority of the exhibits at the Exhibition Rooms, St Andrew's Broad Street, Norwich, employed sensitised paper negatives and contact printing in

5   Thomas Damant Eaton, 1845

printing frames; the process was liable to fade and gave a soft outline. Collodion wet plates (introduced 1851) produced a much sharper result, but the plates had to be exposed and developed before their surface had dried and hardened. In this medium at the exhibition, local member James Howes 'exhibits a copy of some ancient records which in point of sharpness would not disgrace Dr Diamond himself'.

HUGH WELCH DIAMOND

Hugh Welch Diamond (1809–86) was educated at Norwich School from about 1818–24, later being made an honorary member of the Norwich Photographic Society. He showed five calotypes and six collodions at

6   Hugh Welch Diamond. Self portrait *c.* 1855

the 1856 exhibition. The former included, according to the local press review, 'the magnificent "Celtic Cranium from a tumulus" ', the latter 'the famous portraits of the insane', prints from which were recently deposited in the Norfolk and Norwich Record Office by its Chairman, Alderman T. C. Eaton, great-grandson of the Society's President, who doubtless acquired them, along with Dr Diamond's self-portrait (6) after the exhibition. Son of a surgeon, Diamond became a pupil at the Royal College of Surgeons in 1828, but later specialised in mental illness. He was Superintendent of female patients at Surrey County Asylum, Wandsworth (1848–58) and later founded his own private asylum at Twickenham. From 1853–63 he was the Secretary of the London Photographic Society, later editor of its *Journal*. His extensive contributions to *Notes and Queries* included valuable papers on the collodion processes (vol. v) and on the calotype (vol. viii). 'Of his improvements in the practice of photography', states the *Athenaeum*, 'perhaps the most noteworthy at the present time was the substitution of the familiar *cartes-de-visite* for the less convenient 'positives on glass', which were the only photographs supplied to the public till Diamond adopted the mode of printing the 'positives' on paper and then mounting the paper prints on cardboard. Whilst photography was rising to a place amongst the so-called industrial arts, Diamond, without fee or any thought of material reward, acted as scientific instructor to the increasing number of persons who were from different motives interested in the new art'. Ten of Diamond's Norfolk friends, including four of the 1856 exhibitors, wrote in 1853 to *Notes and Queries*: 'We, the undersigned amateurs of Photography in the city of Norwich, shall be obliged if you will . . . convey to Dr Diamond our grateful thanks for the frankness and liberality with which he has published the valuable results of his experiments in the pages of *Notes and Queries*. We have profited largely by Dr Diamond's instructions, and beg to express our conviction that he is entitled to the gratitude of every lover of the Art.'

PETER HENRY EMERSON

Apart from Diamond, two other nationally-regarded photographers have had Norfolk connections. Peter Henry Emerson (1856–1936)(7) was born in Cuba, trained as a physician in England, but gave up practicing in 1886 for many other interests, most notably the rural life of the Fenlands and Broads of East Anglia. No one has more comprehensively and naturalistically photographed a human subject in action. *Life and Landscape on the Norfolk Broads* (with T. F. Goodall, 1886) shows his work at its best, the figures on the 40 platinotypes being dominant and

7   Peter Henry Emerson, 1921

unselfconscious, even if carefully posed. For his next two works Emerson experimented, not always successfully, with different etching processes – *Pictures from life in field and fen* (1887), and *Pictures of East Anglian life* (1888). In the former Emerson stated his credo: 'As a means of artistic expression the camera is second only to the brush . . . . All we ask is that the results should be fairly judged by the only true standard – nature.' One of Emerson's techniques was the use of differential focussing to achieve soft outlines. He was one of the first photographers to publish extensive portfolios of his work, and claimed that *Birds, Beasts and Fishes of the Norfolk Broadland* (1895) was the first book on natural history entirely illustrated by photographs. A man of many idiosyncracies who did not hesitate to criticize his fellow practitioners in the photographic journals, he became so incensed at the limits to which some of them carried naturalistic photography as to publish the extreme *The Death of Naturalistic photography* (1890). His last large-scale photographic work, *Wild life on a Tidal Water,* published in that year with T. F. Goodall, with 30 photo-etchings, reflects his change of heart. For the next 40 years Emerson occupied himself with pictorial processing, short story writing, billiards and genealogy, and resided mainly in the south of England. He produced illustrations 1 and 119.

PAUL MARTIN

Paul Martin (1864–1942) was a Londoner who took up photography in 1884 as a hobby while apprenticed to a firm of wood engravers which executed many of the ubiquitous artists' drawings that filled *The Graphic, The Queen, Illustrated London News,* and the popular Cassell publications of the period, many appearing in parts. In 1904 he became a freelance professional photographer, and is regarded as the first of the candid cameramen, the ordinary public, and not the scenic background, comprising his subject. His technique was possible because of the introduction of hand-held cameras when dry plates succeeded the wet collodion process in the 'seventies and 'eighties. A good deal of Martin's work was done on holiday at Great Yarmouth; illustrations 106 and 155 are examples of his beach scenes there, taken completely without the knowledge of their subjects.

CONCLUSION

Photography, including its fair share of record work, continues to flourish in Norfolk as elsewhere, the present Norwich and District Photographic Society having been established in 1903. Many small

8   Walter John Clutterbuck, 1893

tradesmen have done excellent work in Norfolk; John Melton of Litcham, whose prints are held by the Norfolk County Library, and Henry Logsdail of King's Lynn, who photographed many of his fellow shopkeepers and others 60 years ago (54, 73, 74, 75, 80, 96, 103, 143, 145, 154) are doubtless typical of others whose work survives unregarded in a pile of glass negatives in a back room. Walter J. Clutterbuck of Marsham (1853–1937) (8), whose 90 albums (examples 60, 67, 86, 91, 121, 132, 157) are in the possession of Mr Bryan Hall at Banningham, emulated Emerson in his naturalistic work, but also took many delightful family scenes, as did the Cresswells and the Keppels, whose albums have been put at my disposal.

Several house magazines of the national firms established in Norfolk make extensive use of photography. Colman's *Carrow Works Almanac* replaced line blocks by photography in 1881 and the firm's house magazine (commenced 1907) has continued the tradition. The national advertising campaigns of the Norwich Union Insurance Societies have always been based on scenic photographs of a high order and Jarrolds of Norwich print a high proportion of the British publishing industry's output of photographically illustrated books, especially those using colour. With its great variety of urban and rural scenery Norfolk has indeed been a popular subject for photographers, and one of the incidental satisfactions of compiling this book has been the opportunity afforded me of discovering unknown fresh photographic sources in and out of Norfolk and in several cases of obtaining additional prints for the Norwich Public Libraries' collections.

CITY

9 'A fine old City, truly, is that, view it from whatever side you will; but it shows best from the East'

– George Borrow; *Lavengro*

This Norwich view of 1896 shows on the horizon, left to right, beyond the river, the Castle (14), St. Peter Mancroft Church (10) and the Cathedral, commenced in 1096

10 Norwich Market Place in 1854, by G. R. Fitt, the year the statue of Wellington (*left centre*) was erected. It was removed to the Cathedral Close in 1937. St. Peter Mancroft Church acquired pinnacles in 1883; part of the building in front of it is now the Sir Garnet Wolseley Inn

13 (*opposite*) Davey Place, a pedestrian way from the Market Place to the Castle, was built in 1812. Tyce's Victorian cast-ironwork building was destroyed in 1960 (far left). A Crown post office now stands on the right

11 The Guildhall, seat of Norwich government from the fifteenth to the twentieth centuries, at the North end of the Market Place, in 1845 (*T. D. Eaton*) before the addition of the clock.

12 The Guildhall in 1870, after the curious Renaissance portico had been removed, and the windows altered. The Oxford hotel has taken the place of the Guildhall hotel, along with municipal offices not on the picture. This second development was replaced by war memorial gardens in the nineteen-thirties

14 (*previous page*) In this 1879 view of the twelfth-century Castle the new appearance of the prison development of 1825 on the right, the drovers' Churchillian bowlers, and the Norwich schoolboys' mortarboards give an antique flavour to a scene that changed little until 1960, when the Cattle Market was moved to Harford Bridges. Since 1894 the Castle has housed one of the finest provincial museums

15 The Norwich Corn Hall, built 1861; demolished in 1964, it deserves a place in this brief representation of Norwich occupations. Throughout its life the charge for a stand remained unchanged by act of Parliament at six guineas annually. Dog and flower shows, wrestling and concerts were among the activities which took place there, though the general public knew it best from the Wednesday auctions. The Saturday business in barley, oats and seeds moved to the new Harford Bridges Market in 1963. The portraits in this Edwardian photograph are of the founder, John Culley (1769–1857) and of the agriculturalist, Coke of Holkham (1752–1842)

16 Lamberts, founded 1843, were tea blenders before they diversified into food and tobacco retailing. 'See ThaT you geT good Tea and do noT be led away To buy The rubbish so ofTen offered To The public by unprincipled dealers', they proclaimed around 1904 when this Goat Lane warehouse picture was taken

17 Norwich had no university until 1963, but its Grammar School was probably founded by 1240. The 1855 photograph by G. R. Fitt shows J. F. C. Vincent, headmaster 1852–9, with a group of boys at the School porch in the Cathedral Close. Dr Vincent was later dismissed because 'boys have been placed for hours between shelves so constricted that they cannot stand upright, but are obliged to stoop until the head is brought level with the knees'. The Norwich School is still on and adjoining its original site

18 Crookes Place Board School, later renamed after Sir Samuel Bignold (1792–1875), four times Mayor of Norwich, and chief executive of the Norwich Union Insurance Societies for 60 years. The dark paint, fire guard, Imperialist pictures and glazed screens between classes are characteristic of Board Schools in the early years of the century. Edward Peake is the teacher

19 Carrow School flourished between 1857 and 1919, being founded by Jeremiah James Colman, Norwich's greatest Victorian manufacturer, and a pioneer of industrial paternalism (113, 151)

20 The Managing Director's room, Wincarnis works, 1913 (now Coleman's, wine merchants). Male secretaries, lights on weighted pulleys, open fires and framed diplomas are characteristic of the period, but the shade from the reading lamp was probably removed by the photographer

21 Buntings Corner, St Stephen's Street and Rampant Horse Street, about 1905. Nothing now remains except St Stephen's Church Tower (*far right*). Marks and Spencers' building now occupies the corner site

22 Some Victorian and Edwardian Norwich scenes have changed in the last 25 years. The Pagoda in Chapel Field Gardens, shown in an early First World War photograph, was originally an exhibit by Barnards, iron-mongers, at the Philadelphia Centennial, 1876. It was demolished in 1949, and the bandstand is rarely used now. It was in Chapel Field Gardens, facing his home, that T. D. Eaton took some of the earliest Norwich photographs

23 Cattle no longer roam through Central Norwich, past St George's, Colegate, to the Castle Hill Market (14)

24 (*opposite*) London Street, photographed in 1908, became Norwich's main shopping street in the nineteenth century. It is now a pedestrian way

25 The 1903 edition of Ratcliff's *Drink map of Norwich* records 615 licensed houses, these including breweries, fully licensed houses and beer houses. Norwich pubs varied in style and included this flamboyantly decorated Central Norwich example, which has disappeared

26   The unpretentious Rose Valley inn on Unthank Road which has flourished for well over a century

TOWNS

27   Until the Trades Descriptions Act of 1968 Great Yarmouth and Gorleston-on-Sea proclaimed themselves as 'the resorts that have everything', no misnomer, perhaps, for an ancient fortified town, a safe harbour for merchant and pleasure craft, a modern popular family resort with employment potential in brewing and food processing, and with exceptional literary and historical connections. Still more typical until the last War were over 200 Yarmouth rows, alleys built for economy and as a protection against the weather, up which the fisher folk trundled their catches on narrow troll carts. Few survive; this is Row 60 in 1908

28 'The finest quay in England, if not in Europe. . . . The ships rode here so close, as it were keeping up one another, with their heads fast on shore, that for half a mile together they go across the stream with their bowsprits over the land'.

– Daniel Defoe

29 This view which, like 28, dates from the eighteen-sixties, shows (*right*) the fine trees which once fringed the quay, and also the old classical style Town Hall of 1715

30 Sixty years ago the Scots fisher fleet arrived in Great Yarmouth each October, and in 1913 1,163 boats caught 800,000 crans of herring, a cran being 1,132 fish. By the late nineteen-fifties the catches had declined to around 20,000 crans; only five drifters came in 1968 and none at all in 1969. The gutting and packing was nearly all done by girls

31 Taken in 1903 from a similar vantage point to 29. The character of the shipping has changed little, but the pleasure boats, horse bus, electric tram and Town Hall of 1882 are present. The Haven Bridge was replaced in 1930, and railway, trams and sailing ships have gone now

32 (*overleaf*) A century ago 900 fishing vessels plied from Great Yarmouth and boatyards fringed both sides of the Harbour, turning out wooden craft similar to this one in Hewitt's dock

33 In 1900 Great Yarmouth boasted 16 windmills, including this High Mill at Cobholm, tallest in England, 135 feet high including the lantern at the top. Demolished in 1904, its site is marked today by two houses with red chimney pots. There are now no working windmills in Norfolk

34 Great Yarmouth's three piers have been destroyed, damaged and modified many times over the centuries. Oldest is the Jetty, dating from 1560, where Nelson landed twice. The Wellington pier opened in 1854, and the Britannia pier, here shown at the turn of the century, in 1858

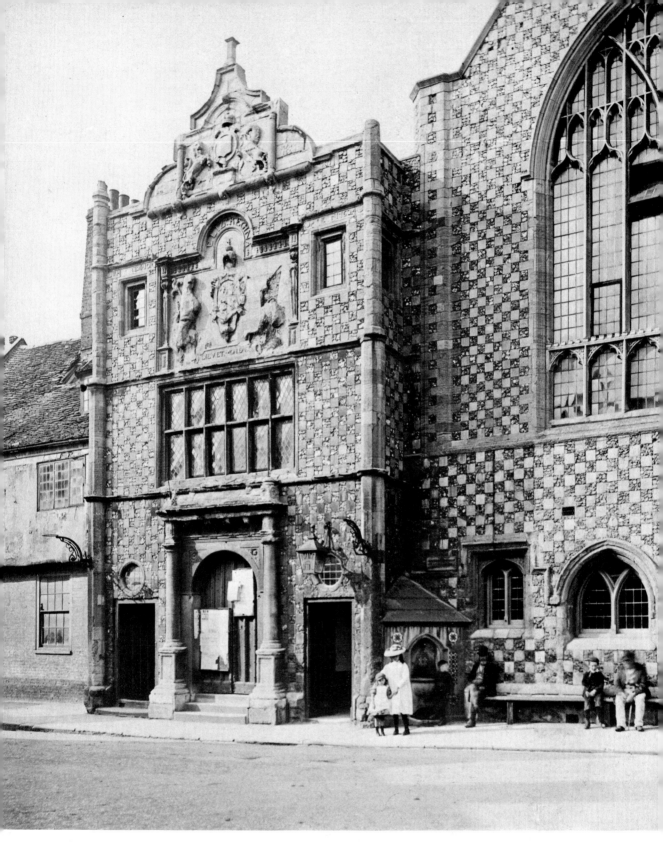

35 Now the third Norfolk town in size, and a festival centre, King's Lynn has fine old civic and commercial buildings, and almost every street bears signs of its former merchandising importance. The Trinity Guildhall dates from about 1580
In 1895–6 matching extensions were added on the West for use as a Town Hall (*left*) shortly after this picture was taken

36 The Custom House, built by Henry Bell in 1683. Thomas Peatling and Sons, established 1826 (now Peatling and Cawdron) still store wines on Purfleet Quay

37 The Alexandra dock, King's Lynn, opened in 1869 by the Prince and Princess of Wales. Its main trade was originally with grain and timber ships from the Baltic. This and the newer Bentinck dock are now fully modernised with roll-on roll-off facilities

38 Thetford was the capital of the kingdom of East Anglia in the Saxon era and the see of a bishop from 1072 until its transfer to Norwich in 1094. This view of St. Peter's Church, fortunately now by-passed by London traffic, has not greatly changed in 60 years, despite the modernisation of the Bell Hotel

39 In South Norfolk, Thetford is rivalled by nearby Diss. By the eighteen-sixties the Mere, after which the town was named, had already attracted around it several residences and the distinctive Baptist Chapel (*right*), erected in 1860

40 A bazaar in Diss Corn Hall in 1864 in aid of the church and school at Heywood, a suburb of Diss. Present are the Revd Charles R. Manning, a noted antiquary who was Rector of Diss 1857–99, his wife and family

41 One of Norfolk's numerous smaller market towns. East Dereham, where the poet William Cowper is buried, here seen *en fête* in 1898

42   The Market Cross in the centre of Wymondham was built in 1616, and served for many years until the first World War as a public reading room and library

TRANSPORT

43 The old Haven bridge, Great Yarmouth, about 1900, with cab, horse bus
from South Town to the Jetty, Midland Railway truck and steamer contributing
to the animated transport scene

44 By the eighteen-nineties the pneumatic tyred, free-wheeling safety bicycle had superseded the penny farthing, which had never been suitable for ladies. The tricycle could be ridden in long skirts, as shown on this group of the family and friends of Frederick Ducker of 130 Alexandra Road, Norwich

45 Longwater lane rustic bridge, Costessey, probably in the eighteen-eighties. Twenty-five years later it had been replaced by a more conventional bridge. Open traps and dog carts of the kind shown negotiating the ford continued in use until well into the twentieth century

46 C. H. Cannell progressed from labouring to a coal round in the early years of the century, fetching his load from Drayton station, 2 miles away. The colloquial spelling of Costessey is somewhat unusual in a printed sign

47 Piped water is still by no means universal in Norfolk. Well water was sold to Shotesham cottagers by the pail from a pony-drawn zinc tank early in the twentieth century

48 For carriage of goods the Norfolk wherry, with its characteristic black sail, had driven the square-sailed keel off the county's inland waterways by the early nineteenth century, but none is now actively at work. This wherry is unloading timber at Surlingham on the Yare near Norwich

50 (*overleaf*) The distant tug is hauling the fisher fleet out of Gorleston harbour in 1891

49 Steam paddle tugs such as the Yare were employed to pull the becalmed fisher fleet out to sea

51 Great Eastern Railway local passenger train pulling into Cromer High Station shortly after its opening in 1877. The station was demolished and the site cleared in the nineteen sixties

52 One of four mustard trains despatched from Carrow works by the G.E.R. on a single day in September, 1895

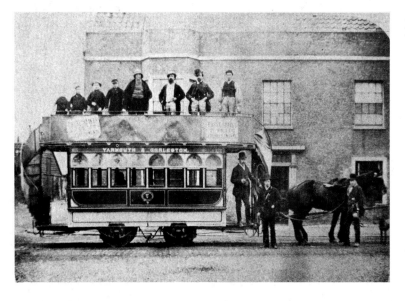

53 This horse-tram plied between Yarmouth Haven Bridge and Gorleston up to 1903

54 (*opposite*) Two proud King's Lynn motor cyclists, about 1907. Vehicles were first numbered in 1903. This one bears a Cambridge registration number (*H. Logsdail*)

55   Norwich's first electric tram at Stump Cross, 1901

56 Frederick Gunton, builder, of Costessey, with his brother William and their wives, visiting East Tuddenham in his new car, purchased in 1905

58 (*overleaf*) The future Sir Henry Jerningham, in frock coat, with his wife, with umbrella, entertaining African visitors outside Costessey Hall (now demolished) about 1910

57 Mr and Mrs C. A. Cresswell driving with friends outside Blakeney Church, 1905

59 The first flight in East Norfolk, August 3rd, 1912, by B. C. Hucks. His Blériot monoplane, the *Firefly,* flew from Crowhurst Farm, Gorleston

THE COAST

60   A Sheringham fisherman, 1894 (*W. J. Clutterbuck*)

61   (*overleaf*) Trips in the bay, portable chairs, bathing machines and an unrivalled remedy for constipation spelled
pleasure enough for these 1894 Great Yarmouth beach crowds

62 Among the North Norfolk resorts, Cromer led the way in fashion and population (1891:2,197) in the later Victorian period. Dominating the foreshore is the Hotel de Paris, whose enlargement in 1894 is being celebrated on this photograph. Opened in 1844, it was in its early days patronised by the German Royal family

63 Jetty Street leads directly from Cromer Church to the Hotel de Paris and the front, and was a fashionable parade centre for the ladies after Sunday morning service

64 Donkey riding was permissible for ladies, riding sidesaddle, in the 'eighties

65 Cromer in 1890 before the modern promenade was built and the Hotel de Paris modernised. The rounded beach pebbles seen being gathered are still useful building material. Both these pictures show Cromer jetty, destroyed by a storm in 1897 and replaced by the present pier in 1901

66 At Sheringham the fishing village has never been completely overshadowed by the resort. The group dates from 1906

67 A Sheringham fisherwoman, 1894 (*W. J. Clutterbuck*)

68 High Street has changed little since this general view of 1906. The pebble in-filling of the 1862 drinking fountain is characteristic of North Norfolk

69 (*overleaf*) Wells-next-the-Sea is one of the best known smaller resorts of North Norfolk. It was once an important port, and was later noted for whelks and mussels

70 The provision of a railway link with King's Lynn and the purchase of Sandringham by the Prince of Wales in the 'sixties contributed to the development of Hunstanton which faces West and has always drawn much of its custom from the Midlands. This general view of 1887 does not extend to the fascinating multi-coloured cliffs

71 Blakeney: the High Street, *c.* 1900

SHOPS AND MARKETS

72 The Royal Arcade, Norwich, early twentieth century, 'with the attached pub on the left is a spectacular display of English Arts and Crafts, when, in spirit though not in form, it came nearest to Continental Art Nouveau: coloured tiles with flower and tree motifs, tracery of a fat, curly Gothicky kind, lettering that could not be made more telling'. The pub has now gone
– Sir Nikolaus Pevsner

73 William Ely's baker's and confectioner's shop and catering establishment, 4 Norfolk Street, King's Lynn, in 1907, with the manageress, Laura Rowe. The shop closed in 1960 (*Henry Logsdail*)

74 The Penny Bazaar, King's Lynn, *c.* 1907 (*Henry Logsdail*)

75 Mrs Louisa Brooke's glass and china warehouse, 147 Norfolk Street, King's Lynn, 1907 (*Henry Logsdail*)

76 White Lion Street, Norwich, about 1905. Although changes are not obvious, after 60 years every occupancy is different except the Castle Hotel, visible at the end of the street

77 The shop of Signor Henri Aegena, artist, photographer and picture-frame-maker, flourished at 11 White Hart Street, Thetford, from the mid-seventies to the mid-'eighties

78 John Ebenezer Hall, Saddler, Reepham Market Place, with his staff, in 1912. The bow front was later removed, and the shop is now a butcher's

79 Church Street, Cromer, in 1900. The ladies are looking in the windows of Thomas Mack, jet cutter, photographer and optician

80 Adcock and Son, tobacconists, 112 High Street, King's Lynn, probably in 1907. The twopenny 'sure shot' cigar was very popular at this period (*Henry Logsdail*)

81 The Tuesday Market Place, King's Lynn, about 1905. Centre is the Corn Exchange (1854) described by Pevsner as 'jolly and vulgar'. The lamp post on the right marks the site of the Market Cross, demolished 1831

82 Great Yarmouth Market Place in the eighteen-eighties. The parish church of St Nicholas, one of the largest in England, was completely gutted in 1942, and its spire has not been restored

COUNTRY HOUSES

83 Norfolk, with its fair share of major stately homes, is unsurpassed in the number of those of more modest size. Westwick House, restored about 1800, was the home of John Berney Petre, who died in 1882, shortly after this photograph was taken

84 A royal group in Commodore Wood, Sandringham, November 1909. It includes King Edward VII and Queen Alexandra, future kings George V, Edward VIII and George VI, along with the later Queen Mary, Mary the Princess Royal, and the Duke of Gloucester

85 Sandringham House, Norfolk, purchased by the Prince of Wales in 1862, and afterwards rebuilt, has been the favourite country home of several members of the royal family. The Princess of Wales filled her drawing room with gifts and souvenirs until it was over-flowing

86 Sir Henry Jacob Preston (1851–97) and his wife Mary Hope (d. 1925) boating on the lake at his seat, Beeston St Lawrence Hall, on July 15th 1887. Photograph by W. J. Clutterbuck, Lady Preston's brother

87 The Gurneys of Norfolk fill six pages of the 1965 *Landed Gentry*. Those depicted here are descendants of Daniel Gurney (1791–1880), of North Runcton Hall, near King's Lynn, brother of Elizabeth Fry, the prison reformer. Daniel's second son, William Hay Gurney, took the family living of North Runcton and married Anna Maria, always known as Ama, the eldest daughter of the Squire of Ketteringham (89), shown in pensive mood with her son Mortimer Hay Gurney (1855–1925) about 1880

88 None of the three Gurneys in this North Runcton Hall picture lived to be 55. Hugh (1867–1913) and Muriel (d. 1907) are brother and sister; their second cousin Anselm (1864–1916), next to a young friend of the family, is brother to Mortimer Hay Gurney (87)

89 Group at Ketteringham Hall, owned by Sir John Boileau (1794–1869). Life at Ketteringham is described in *Victorian miniature* by Owen Chadwick (1960), who tells of Sir John's greatest embarrassment. Thinking his wife was dying in 1853 he had a number of bodies from a vault in Ketteringham Church chancel exhumed to make space for her, believing them to have been there for centuries, only to receive an angry letter from a Cambridge landowner claiming that one was his sister-in-law! Sir John had to have all the corpses put back. This picture was taken after his wife was buried in 1862 – in the churchyard, and not under the chancel

90 Although the population of Knapton, North Walsham, remained around 300 for most of the nineteenth century, the village sustained three large houses. Knapton New Hall, now a hotel, was a private residence when this 1906 photograph was taken

92 (*opposite*) The guest hall of Carrow Priory, now a lounge for executives at Carrow Works, where the Colman library (*see* introduction) was housed in the late nineteenth century

91 The drawing room of Northrepps Cottage, near Cromer, in 1893, home of Mr and Mrs W. J. Clutterbuck before they moved to Marsham Hall. It is now a restaurant

93 The Rev. John Edwards (1790–1832) of Hardingham Hall was survived by his widow for 41 years. She was Lucy Marsham of Stratton Strawless Hall and is shown in her phaeton in front of Hardingham Hall about 1850

94 (*overleaf*) The outdoor staff of Hardingham Hall about 1860 during the squirearchy of H. W. B. Edwards (1820–1909), grandfather of the present owner, Sir Bartle Edwards, Chairman of Norfolk County Council, 1950–66

95 The Hon. Arnold Keppel, afterwards the 8th Earl of Albemarle (1858–1942) took this group at Eccles Hall, Attleborough, dower house to the family seat in Quidenham, two miles away, in the late 'eighties. It includes (*left*) his sister, the future Lady Theodora Davidson (d. 1945), his wife, and their guests who were to become Sir Francis Astley-Corbett, Bt., and Lady Gertrude Astley-Corbett

96 The followers of the West Norfolk hounds, Gayton Hall, Norfolk, in November 1908 included King Edward and Queen Alexandra, their daughter-in-law the Princess of Wales (later Queen Mary), and grandchildren Prince Albert and Princess Mary (*Henry Logsdail*)

97   King Edward VII stayed at Quidenham Hall on October 23rd 1909 to review the Territorials at Norwich. Standing behind the King are (*left to right*) the 17th Earl of Derby (1865–1948), R. B. (later Viscount) Haldane, Minister of War (1856–1928), the 8th Earl of Albemarle, and the 3rd Earl of Leicester (1848–1941), Lord Lieutenant. On the King's right is his hostess, Lady Albemarle (d. 1943) and next to her Viscountess Bury (d. 1928), first wife of the present Earl of Albemarle. On the King's left is the Countess of Leicester (d. 1936). Viscount Bury, the present Earl of Albemarle, who has kindly identified these ladies and gentlemen, is on the top left of the group

WORK, LEISURE AND REPOSE

98 Hobrough and Son, established 1854 in Norwich, described as 'general contractors, dredging, pile driving, lighterage, clearing mill dams, etc.' Here their workmen are laying drain pipes at Sheringham in 1909

99 Brickmaking in Costessey developed originally about 1800 to embellish Costessey Hall, and there were later two yards supplying the country at large. Barney brickworks continued in production until the nineteen-sixties. Harry Barnes is here seen moulding coping bricks to top walls and gables. He was paid 22/– for a 58½ hour week and his firm sold each coping for about a penny

100 One of Hobrough's divers exploring the channel at Acle Bridge prior to dredging, about 1900

101 In the middle ages the flesh of the cygnet was greatly esteemed, and breeding of swans was only permitted to those possessing the royal swanmaster's licence. The swan pit at the Great Hospital, Norwich is probably the last to survive. Until the Second World War the Hospital swans used to be plucked, trussed and sent oven-ready with instructions which end as follows:

To a gravy of beef (good and strong) I opine
You'll be right if you add half a pint of port wine:
Pour this through the swan – yes, quite through
*   the belly,*
Then serve the whole up with some hot currant
*   jelly.*

102 The cradle, outsize spanner and safety lamp, point to work inside and outside Norwich Cathedral, probably during the restorations of the eighteen-nineties

103 A blacksmith and his assistant, King's Lynn, about 1907 (*Henry Logsdail*)

104 A sale of cod at the Gangway, Cromer in 1895, by J. J. Davies. He was step-father to Henry Blogg, the lifeboat captain and George Cross holder

105 Roadmenders with brazier and toilet hut in St. Andrew's Street, Norwich, about 1897. The building with the classical façade on the right was erected as the Royal Bazaar in 1831 and ended its days as the Theatre de Luxe, the first Norwich cinema, in 1957. It was demolished in 1971

106 In the nineteenth and early twentieth centuries Norfolk offered first class, easily accessible recreation on the coast, in the country, and in its towns. This intimate beach scene at Great Yarmouth was snapped by Paul Martin in the nineties

107   Poster site in Ber Street, Norwich, 1895, offering a choice of attractions (*H. J. Howard*)

109   (*overleaf*) A picnic in the woods at Felbrigg, North Norfolk, in 1911

108   Roller skating 'patronised by the élite; good music' at the Norwich Agricultural Hall, now the headquarters of Anglia Television, about 1906

110 (*opposite*) The Batley family at the golf links, Caister-on-sea, about 1900. James B. Batley (b. 1876) reached international standard, being one of five brothers, all of whom became golf professionals. Three are on the picture with their mother, grandmother, three boys acting as caddies and an interested spectator carrying a scythe

111 (*opposite*) After establishing itself in the 'sixties as a popular game for both sexes, croquet yielded popularity to tennis on social occasions but was still played at schools and colleges. These girls are at the Norwich Training College in 1901

112 (*opposite*) Norwich City F.C. pressing West Ham United in the Southern League at the Newmarket Road Ground in front of a 7,000 crowd on October 7th, 1905. This was their first professional season, and they won one-nil. Although styled Canaries, the club then played in blue and white halves

113 Funeral of Jeremiah James Colman (1830–98), Norwich's great nineteenth-century industrialist and Liberal M.P. who also found time to establish the great library (92) that has provided material for this book. The heir, Russell J. Colman (1861–1946), H.M. Lieutenant for Norfolk 1929–44, is in the centre of this Rosary cemetery picture

114 Shipwrecks off the Norfolk coast have always been frequent, and lifeboats from Caister have rescued more men than those from elsewhere. On November 14th 1901 nine crew were lost, three others being saved by James Haylett, a 78-year-old ex-coxswain, who in reply to a question at the inquest stated 'Caister lifeboatmen never turn back'

COUNTRY PURSUITS

115 Mr Howard of Hilborough, Norfolk, in his smock after 45 years as a shepherd. This photograph commemorates Mr and Mrs Howard's golden wedding

116 (*overleaf*) Threshing tackle owned by Stephen Dane of North Tuddenham driven by a traction engine in 1912. Such engines were made in Thetford, Norfolk, from 1856

117 Despite women's lib. there are fewer British women landworkers than there were 50 years ago, or than there are on the European continent today. These Norfolk harvesters, photographed about 1900, are wearing old-fashioned sun bonnets

118 Oxen were used in agriculture in Norfolk until well into the present century. This photograph dates from 1889

119 P. H. Emerson's *Pictures from life in Field and Fen* (1887) reproduces his photograph of a dame school in the heart of Norfolk far from the nearest Board school

120 Robert Brown, aged 72, riding a wooden tricycle made by James Patteson of Foxley about 1875 on the Bawdeswell Road, Foxley, August 1915

121 A wet day in the 'nineties at a North Norfolk market (*W. J. Clutterbuck*)

BROADS AND RIVERS

122   Long before the Broads were popularised as a holiday venue by Christopher
Davies, later Clerk of Norfolk County Council, in *The Swan and her crew*
(1876), they had provided a living for many marsh dwellers such as the couple
trapping eels near their reed boat house (c. 1900)

123–125 Broads holiday traffic was almost wholly by rail within our period and Wroxham (123) and the Great Eastern Railway always held a lead over Potter Heigham and the Midland and Great Northern (124, across). Horning (125, across) was never on a railway. Absence of today's motor-boats and of bungaloid growth is the most notable feature of all these three pictures of the Broads district; 'in a journey through it by rail, you see nothing but its flatness; walk along its roads, you see the dullest side of it; but take to its water-highways, and the glamour of it steals over you if you have aught of the love of nature, the angler or the artist in you'. (*G. Christopher Davies*)

126 The boundaries of the City of Norwich extend several miles down the River Yare to Hardley Cross. Councillors and officials are shown carrying out a periodical inspection, perhaps an excuse for a pleasant outing, in the eighteen-eighties

127   The Hobrough family and friends cruising on the Broads about 1900

OCCASIONS

128 During festivities the characteristic Norfolk restraint quite disappears, and Queen Victoria's two jubilees added much colour to the local scene. R. H. Mottram describes this Norwich Market Place balloon ascent of June 22nd, 1897. 'Stephen had, of course, never seen, even less entered such a contrivance, but it was bound to be safe if Father took him. He gave no further thought to the matter, sat where he was bid in a queer receptacle like an enormous laundry basket, the small band in attendance struck up the lively air expected of it, some one did something to the machinery, and they began to mount'. (*Castle Island*, p. 171). (*H. J. Howard*)

129 Of this distribution of 1470 joints of Australian meat in St. Andrew's Hall, Norwich on Jubilee day 1897 it was said 'generally speaking the recipients belonged obviously to the lower working classes, but there were a few who wore an air of faded respectability'

130 Service in the Primitive Methodist chapel, Blo Norton, Norfolk, about 1895

131 During their stay at Sandringham the Victorian Royal family worshipped in turn at all the churches on the estate, as do their successors today. In 1868 the Princess of Wales (1844–1925) accompanied the future Duke of Clarence (1864–92) and George V (1865–1936) to Hillingdon church

Princess of Wales with Prince Victor & Prince George 1868

132 (*opposite*) Preparing for the service at Sloley, about 1895 (*W. J. Clutterbuck*)

133 Sartorial contrasts at the opening of the Borrow House Museum, Norwich, July 5th, 1913. Now a Council house marked by a plaque, Borrow's mother wrote of it: 'I wish my dear George would not have such fancies about the old house; it is a mercy it has not fallen on my head before this'

134 The only existing photograph of George Borrow, taken in 1848. Borrow (1803–81), born at East Dereham, was the most eminent literary figure in Norfolk in the nineteenth century

135 The Queen's Jubilee celebrations at North Walsham, 1887

136 Banquet at Norwich's oldest hotel, the Maid's Head, 5th July, 1913, attended by Augustine Birrell, Sir Sidney Lee and Clement K. Shorter. No Norwich literary celebration since has surpassed it

137 Prince of Wales Road, Norwich, in readiness for King Edward VII, November 26th, 1909

138 The Cringleford bridge disaster of September 4th 1901 involved two racing traction engines, one plunging over the parapet into the River Yare with two fatalities. The snapshot by H. J. Howard shows the recovery of the engines on the following day

139 On August 24th 1854 this workhouse, originally a chapel-at-ease to St Margaret's Church, King's Lynn, fell, killing two persons

140 (*overleaf*) The Norwich flood of August 26th 1912 was probably the greatest disaster ever inflicted on the city, though only two lives were lost. These men are light-heartedly clearing up in Magdalen Street

141 District tea in 1904 in the grounds of the Garden House, Beaconsfield Parade, New Hunstanton, home of Col G. F. A. (1852–1926) and Mrs Cresswell

142 King's Lynn Theatre Royal, originally opened in 1815 was modernised in 1904 for this gala reopening on September 26th. It was burned down in 1936

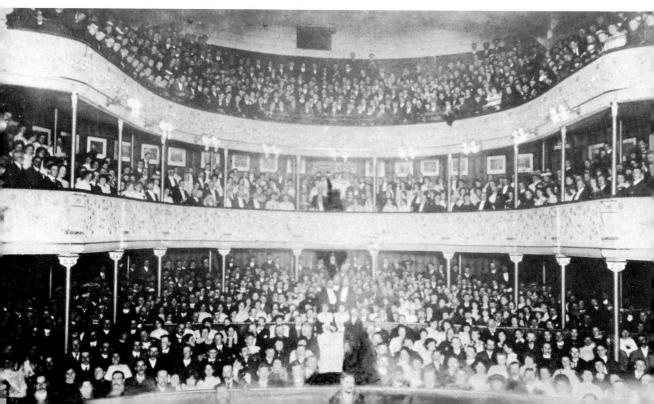

143 In 1905 S. G. Street's music warehouse, Beethoven House, King's Lynn, advertised an agency for gramophones and Madame Melba's records. This picture dates from 1907 (*Henry Logsdail*)

144 The opening of King's Lynn Public Library by Andrew Carnegie, May 18th 1905

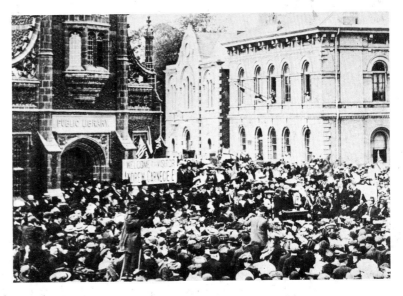

145 Catholic pilgrimage to Walsingham passing King's Lynn Public Library, 1907 (*Henry Logsdail*)

146 Empire day in Watton, May 24th 1907, a festival inaugurated in 1902 by the Earl of Meath to train school children in good citizenship. This is now commemorated as Commonwealth day on the Queen's official birthday

147 Long Stratton Friendly societies' church parade, July 28th 1907

148 The annual round of fairs in Norfolk, many granted by Royal charter, begins on St Valentine's Day, February 14th, on the King's Lynn Tuesday Market Place. This 1905 picture shows the Mayor (Ald. E. Dunn) at the customary civic opening of the Fair

149 The *Eastern Evening News* printed special bills to announce the treat given to its paper boys at the Norwich Hippodrome in 1905

150 Unveiling by Lord Avebury of the statue of Sir Thomas Browne by Henry Pegram, the Haymarket, Norwich, October 19th 1905

151 Carrow workpeople's fête to celebrate the coming of age of Russell J. Colman (with cane), Sept. 5th, 1882. (See also no. 113). J. J. Colman is also on the picture

152 (*overleaf*) The Essex Regiment marching down London Street, Norwich, April 5th

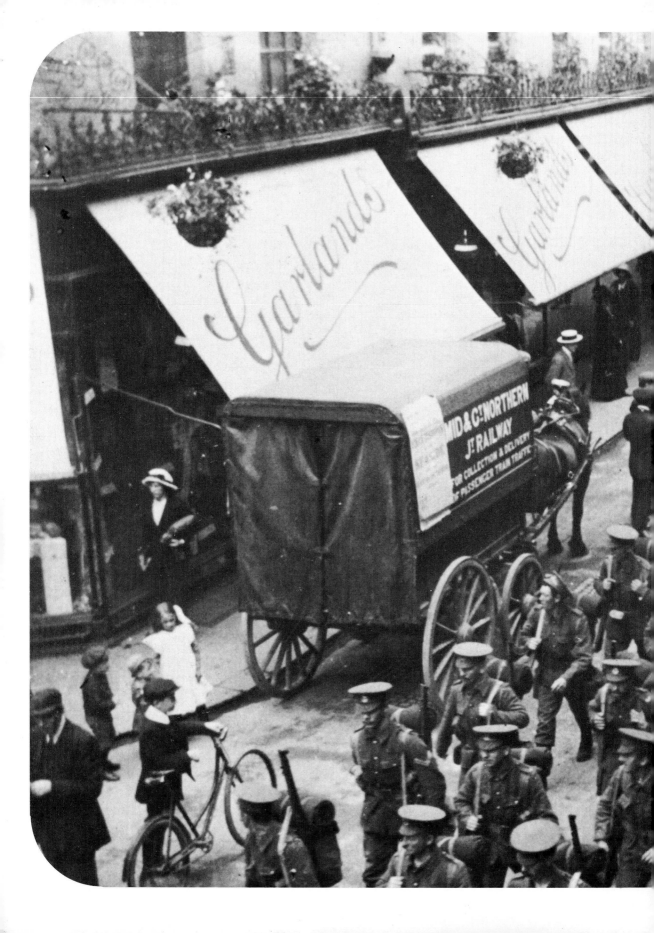

153　Suffragettes in Prince of Wales Road, Norwich

CHILDREN

154   This charming 1907 King's Lynn study, by Henry Logsdail, of a small boy with father and grandfather raises the inevitable question – what became of him?

155 (*overleaf*) Yarmouth sands in the 'nineties (*Paul Martin*)

156 North Norfolk woods, 1909

157 Jacob and Eddie Preston tending a bonfire at Hill House, Northrepps, in March 1894. The boys became Sir Jacob Preston, 4th Bt (1887–1918) and Sir Edward Preston, 5th Bt (1888–1963), High Sheriff of Norfolk, 1956, of Beeston St Lawrence Hall (*W. J. Clutterbuck*)

158 *Cartes-de-visite* were normally used for individual portraiture and it was difficult in the sixties to ensure that the littlest ones kept absolutely still for the fairly lengthy exposure

159 Performing bear, Earlham Road Norwich, early twentieth century

160 Ready for a ride in a goat cart in Norwich, 1897

I heard this day bird after bird –
But not one like the child has heard.
A hundred butterflies saw I –
But not one like the child saw fly.
I saw the horses roll in grass –
But no horse like the child saw pass.
My world this day has lovely been –
But not like what the child has seen.

W. H. Davies

161 Burston, near Diss, was in 1914 the scene of a strike of schoolchildren protesting against the dismissal of their headmistress and her husband. A rival school was built by public subscription in 1917 'to protest against the action of the Education authorities, to provide a free school, to be a centre of rural democracy and a memorial of the villagers' fight for freedom'

162 Peter Cuthbert Cresswell (1886–1952) and Jo Cresswell in 1889, photographed against the inevitable scenic canvas background. Captain Francis Joseph Cresswell (1883–1914), father of Lady Harrod who loaned this picture, was killed at Mons, one of the first British officers lost in the Great War